COMPACT LIVING

JANE GRAINING

COMPACT LIVING

SOMA

For John Reeve

First published 1999 in Great Britain by Mitchell Beazley,
an imprint of Octopus Publishing Group Limited. North
American edition published 1999 by Soma Books, by
arrangement with Mitchell Beazley.

Soma Books is an imprint of Bay Books & Tapes,
555 De Haro St., No. 220, San Francisco, CA 94107.

For the Mitchell Beazley edition:
Commissioning Editor: Judith More
Executive Art Editor: Janis Utton
Project Editor: Stephen Guise
Editor: Jane Donovan
Design: Pike
Special Photography: Dominic Blackmore
Illustration: The Maltings Partnership
Production: Rachel Stavely
Index: Sue Farr

For the SOMA edition:
North American Editor: Karen O'Donnell Stein
Production: Jeff Brandenburg

Library of Congress Cataloging-in-Publication data
on file with the Publisher

ISBN 1-57959-026-8

Printed and bound by Toppan Printing Co., (HK) Ltd.
Produced in China

10 9 8 7 6 5 4 3 2 1

Distributed by Publishers Group West

CONTENTS

6   **INTRODUCTION**

12   **CASE HISTORIES**
     Solo living
     Room for two
     The compact family
     Homeworking

30   **LIVING**
     The framework
     Zoning with color
     Creating space

50   **COOKING AND EATING**
     The framework
     Storage
     Zoning with color
     Creating space
     Display ideas

70   **SLEEPING**
     The framework
     Creating space
     Zoning with color
     Display ideas

86   **BATHING**
     The framework
     Showers
     Bathtubs
     Sinks
     Faucets
     Toilets
     Decorating ideas

104 **WORKING**
     The framework
     Lighting
     Desk areas

114 **SOLUTIONS**
     Heating
     Lighting
     Laundry
     Overflow storage

124 Sources
126 Index
128 Acknowledgments

INTRODUCTION

Today's strong demand for individual living accommodations, combined with high real estate prices, has made the efficient and cost-effective use of space one of the fundamental issues in interior design. Alongside the building of new housing with smaller living units, the conversion of period homes into studios and apartments has been going on for years. Vacant warehouses, old factories, and other industrial buildings are now divided into apartments, and it is apparent that more and more single people and couples are choosing to live in studios and lofts in desirable districts in towns and cities rather than in two-bedroom apartments way out in the suburbs.

Among architects and interior designers there is a keen awareness that space has become a luxury and, consequently, there is a growing desire to find ever more inventive solutions to cope with space limitations. Discussions with designers on how to make the best use of a limited living area result in the same basic approach time and time again: the key to small-space living is flexibility and convertibility. The trick is to increase the efficiency of a space by using it at least twice. Most of us want living and sleeping areas, somewhere to put up the occasional guest, a place to cook and eat, and a place to work, even if it's just somewhere to pay the monthly bills. But each function doesn't necessarily require a separate room.

Compact living is not about creating a series of tiny rooms. Putting up walls and committing yourself to a certain size of table at which to host a dinner party that may happen only once a month is an unaffordable luxury in a small space. It's better to have a smaller table, large enough for a couple of people, that can be extended to entertain more guests, or one that folds away to be recessed into either a wall space or a closet. And it's the same with spare bedrooms. In theory, it's always a good idea to have a guest room to accommodate family and friends when they come to stay, but even if the room is occupied once a month, it is still wasted space for the rest of the time. If the space is turned into a home office or maybe a workroom and is made available for other uses, but has an extra bed stored away, it begins to earn its keep.

Something else to consider is the amount of space designated for circulation. Corridor and hall space in small apartments should be minimized. If the space must be retained, perhaps to comply with fire regulations, make it dual purpose: a table that extends for parties, for example, might open out into a corridor to make better use of space. Compact-living issues are usually about the use of space on one floor and the flow between areas in what are quite often open-plan units. Considered planning, which includes giving thought to which activities merit the lion's share of the space, has to be the first priority. Then there are two main ways of tackling the space. First, keep it as open and clear as possible, and use a minimal amount of furniture so the eye takes in the size of the space and not an excess of detail. Second, divide the space with changes in floor level and designate different areas of activity with screening walls that create the illusion of more space beyond.

Small-space living is best kept uncluttered, so to accommodate all the daily accessories that go with life, plenty of storage is essential. Hide things away where possible, but remember to keep them accessible, too. Whole walls can conceal storage space and beds: disguised behind a façade of doors that integrates it into the structure of the room, a foldaway bed will "read" as wall space.

Top In this city apartment, designed by Circus Architects, a corner of the living area is also used for dining. Between two red "closet" doors, a glass block strip lets light filter into a bathroom under the staircase.

Center Dual-purpose design means that when overnight guests come to stay, the lightweight table and chairs move to one side and the doors swing open to reveal two foldaway twin beds.

Bottom The owners of the apartment bought a mirrored screen with a folding wooden section that is used, along with the "closet" door, to partition off this sleeping space from the main living area.

Left In this tiny unit,
just 130 square feet
including the staircase,
architects AEM created,
through clever use of
horizontal and vertical
space, an airy living area
with assigned locations
for cooking, eating, and
seating. Behind the
metal staircase – it has
storage space on one
side and has been
converted into cabinets
on the other – and below
the bed platform is a
bathroom. Behind this
is a workroom with a
bed that folds into the
wall. Limiting the
materials in the main
living area to white walls
and pale wood helps
to keep the space fresh,
clean, and open.

Above left In a 105-square-foot upstairs apartment in a nineteenth-century house, bathroom, kitchen, and bedroom storage is arranged against a wall in the middle of the space to create an open corridor between the living/eating/working area and the bedroom. Kitchen and study areas (cabinets that can be closed off) face into the living area; folding doors hide the "kitchen" and aluminum blinds conceal the work area.

Above right Kitchen and study cabinets use the full height of the wall to minimize visual distraction. Architect Hugh Broughton used white walls and ceilings, with sisal matting, to enhance the light and space.

When you are planning the use of walls, aim to think vertically as well as horizontally. Low-level storage – units built under beds or seating – makes use of otherwise wasted space. Understair space is ideal for storing awkwardly shaped items such as bicycles and other sports equipment, if it isn't large enough to house a utility room or small home office. Use high-level spaces to hold items that are used only occasionally; they can be accessed via lightweight ladders that fold down and store away. High-ceilinged rooms can often accommodate galleries or lofts – an excellent way of adding a touch of visual drama – which can be utilized as sleeping platforms, study areas, or simply spaces for storage, acting as giant shelves while the areas below are used for other activities.

At the same time, don't neglect or forget about the "dead" space of shallow recesses and awkward corners created (especially in period properties) by architectural features, pipes, and other utilities. These spaces can be filled with shelves for storage or display.

As this book returns to some of these ideas, you will learn that "compact living" demands forethought, self-discipline, and imagination. In those who are up to the creative challenge, it can prompt some marvelously inventive design solutions.

CASE HISTORIES

SOLO LIVING

In a 1930s office building, converted by a property developer into apartments of varying sizes, a busy professional woman has found an urban hideaway that suits her needs exactly.

The unit bought by the current owner was, at 750 square feet, the smallest of the conversions, and the shape of the shell had already been defined. In its raw form the interior possessed all the charm of a parking garage, with concrete floor, ceiling, and support pillar. A red brick wall supported huge new windows that looked in onto bare walls plastered pink. Water, gas, and electric supplies were capped just above the door. The industrial feel of the space, however, was very much part of the unit's appeal, offering the right framework for the simple and contemporary style of design and decoration that the owner knew she wanted.

Today's basic layout is the result of an initial collaboration with Circus Architects and reflects the owner's desire to keep as much space as possible free for an open living area. As a PR executive for an international company, she entertains on a regular, albeit relatively informal, basis; hence, she needs a dining table that is large enough to seat ten comfortably and a kitchen that opens onto the living area. The service rooms – kitchen, bathroom, and dressing room – are all

Left A spare, minimalist approach to furnishing clearly emphasizes the apartment's structural skeleton. The flank wall is divided into several neat sections, with the L-shaped kitchen on one side and a tall storage cabinet on the other. In between is the large box-shaped bathroom with the sleeping area above.

Right The kitchen counter is hidden below the L-shaped bar dividing this area from the rest of the space. Glass tiles in the walls of the bathroom allow natural light in and artificial light out.

Below left Behind the curved screen, a beech pull-up table and wall-mounted mirror (lit by strips of lightbulbs) furnish this satellite of the main dressing room.

Below center A niche in the outer side of the screen holds objets d'art.

Below right The spiral staircase leading to the sleeping deck is made partly of scaffolding tubes.

neatly compacted against the flank wall, with the otherwise dead space above the bathroom ingeniously utilized as a sleeping deck. Natural light filters into the bathroom through glass block panels inset into the walls. The main space itself was barely altered, except for the addition of a curved screen in the corner. Primarily installed to comply with a local building code, the screen creates a focus within the living area and at the same time conceals extra storage.

The light and spacious effect is further enhanced by the materials chosen to furnish the space. Natural shades of pale blond wood for kitchen cabinets and furniture and beech floorboards contrast subtly with the neutral cream and gray of the walls and ceilings. Huge roll-up blinds, which pull up from the bottom, cover the two windows, offering seclusion from the outside world while allowing daylight in.

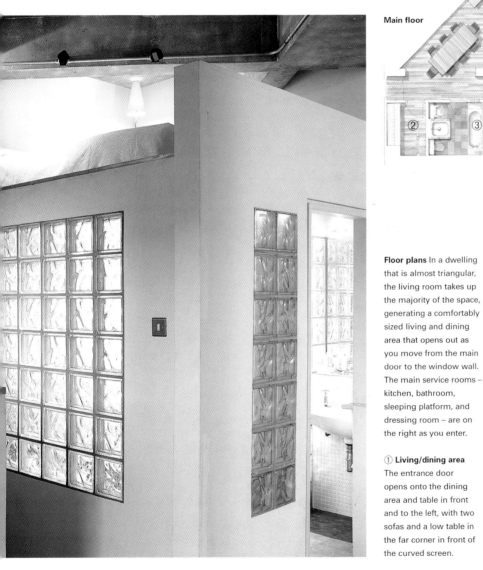

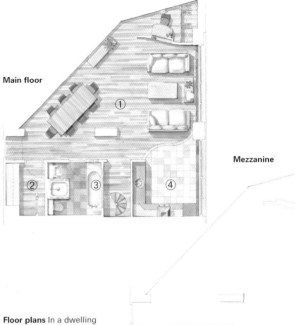

Main floor

Mezzanine

Floor plans In a dwelling that is almost triangular, the living room takes up the majority of the space, generating a comfortably sized living and dining area that opens out as you move from the main door to the window wall. The main service rooms – kitchen, bathroom, sleeping platform, and dressing room – are on the right as you enter.

① **Living/dining area** The entrance door opens onto the dining area and table in front and to the left, with two sofas and a low table in the far corner in front of the curved screen.

② **Dressing room** This room (which holds the central heating system as well) has 12-foot-tall closets for work clothes and shoes, and additional storage space in the cupboards above.

③ **Bathroom** On one side is the bathtub with storage shelves at each end; on the other are the sink and shower that shield the toilet in the corner from view.

④ **Kitchen** This area, which is raised two steps, has a cream stone floor that subtly conveys its separation from the main living/dining area. Storage space has been provided in the form of wall and base cabinets and a refrigerator on the back wall.

⑤ **Sleeping deck** This area holds a double bed and three double storage cabinets.

ROOM FOR TWO

West London is full of stately, elegant Victorian houses that have been converted into studios and apartments. In one of these properties a young couple, eager to live in the area, found a gloomy studio. Previously a rather grand billiard room, the studio had an unworkably small kitchen and an extremely cramped bathroom. The only windows looked out onto the bottom of lightwells between the adjacent buildings, so there was little natural light inside and no view. On the plus side, the studio extended out at the back of the house and had a large horizontal roof above. The couple felt the space had potential, as did architects AEM, who eventually received permission to build an additional story on top.

From these unpromising roots grew a two-bedroom, two-bathroom apartment with a comfortably sized kitchen/diner and a light-filled living area opening out onto a small terrace. The hinge between the floors is a skewed staircase that rises in a single swift flight, acting at the same time as a lightwell. This helps to disperse the gloom on the ground floor, while a generously sized entrance hall establishes an immediate sense of open space. On the right of the entrance door, with a shared window overlooking the lightwell, is a pair of back-to-back bathrooms containing toilet and bathing facilities. On each side of the staircase lies a bedroom, separated by

Right In a now-spacious hall, natural daylight filters down the staircase into the middle of the ground floor. During the evening, upstairs lighting reflects off the ceiling into the hall. Fluorescent fixtures, which are hidden behind the horizontal overhead beam in the hall, wash light over the vaulted brickwork ceiling to help illuminate both the bedroom areas.

Floor plans In this apartment the lower floor, which is darker than the upper floor, is utilized for sleeping quarters, storage space, and bathrooms. A double bathroom and the main bedroom look out onto lightwells.

① **Bedrooms** The entire end wall is lined with closets. An etched glass wall divides the bedrooms, and the staircase wall provides privacy in the sleeping area of the main bedroom.

② **Bathrooms** On one side, the bathtub is slotted into a closet-sized space looking onto the lightwell. On the other side the shower extends slightly into the corner of the second bedroom, creating a neat space for a work table.

③ **Living area** This area possesses ample room for seating and access to the terrace through sliding glass doors. Shelves for storage and display are built on top of the staircase wall to accommodate a TV and stereo equipment.

④ **Kitchen** The staircase separates the cooking and living areas. One wall holds the stove, sink, and storage. A refrigerator and washing machine are inside cabinets on the adjoining wall.

First Floor

Second Floor

an etched glass wall to maximize light levels. The full-height doors to both rooms open to minimize the solid wall area.

Natural light streams through a clear glass wall into the main upper-floor living area, and sliding doors open onto a duckboard terrace lined with plant pots. The staircase walls rise into the upper floor, and good use has been made of their reverse sides. In the living area, the wall becomes a storage unit that holds the TV, audio equipment, and books, while bench seating runs along the kitchen side. With a glass screen above and a pivoting door, this area can be divided off for cooking without losing the sense of space. Inspired use of bold color in a neutral shell — white and brick walls and maple wood floors and lots of glass — works effectively with the architects' spatial solutions to turn the space into a comfortably light apartment.

Top left The skylight from the original studio room was recycled for the new unit in the ceiling above the kitchen.

Top center Below the skylight on the upper level is a glass shelf, allowing light to filter down to the lower level and offering an unexpected view of the hall.

Top right Custom-made storage forms a fixed edge to the stairwell and living area. A deep blue sofa contrasts with and balances the red staircase walls.

Left Sliding glass panels separate the kitchen from the living area.

THE COMPACT FAMILY

For a couple with a child, a converted nineteenth-century schoolhouse provided an opportunity to place a contemporary interior within a traditional structure. When they found it, the unit was just a shell with a small basic mezzanine. The brief to the architects, Granit, was to provide separate sleeping and bathroom facilities while retaining the double-height, open living area that so appealed to the family.

The solution involved ripping out the existing mezzanine and installing a steel structure that created two new upper levels and an open lower floor. Sweeping curves are boldly introduced by a spiral staircase that opens onto a galleried second floor with splayed wooden balustrading. The double-height ceiling soars above the hall, creating drama as you walk in. Beyond is a compact utility area hidden behind doors adjacent to the kitchen. A curved maple counter separates the kitchen from the spacious dining/living area. The counter's curve mirrors the edge of the study's balcony above and fits neatly around the steel structural column at one end, which is also the center of the spiral staircase into the main attic bedroom.

A pitched roof cavity was opened up for the top bedroom's ceiling, and the full width of the room was kept by running oak floorboards out to the apexes where floor and roof meet. The

Left A patchwork of brightly colored tiles in the kitchen creates a strong focus point and balances the impact of the curved wooden balustrade on the galleried landing above. Natural materials in the framework of the building, such as the yellow brick walls and the oak floor, harmonize with the stainless steel structure that dominates the core of the apartment.

expanse of floor gives a feeling of openness. A curved wall opens into a circular bathroom with cylindrical shower and walk-in dressing room/closet. On the middle level, the child's bedroom is just seven feet high, with doors opening onto the balcony and the double-height void of the dining area below. Here, the edge of the sloping roof is concealed by a window seat, and deep cabinets extend to full ceiling height. Opposite, steps lead down into a bathroom to make use of reduced headroom below. At the far end of this level is the open part of the galleried floor with office space.

The materials used give a coordinated look. New and old oak floors, ash doors, exposed yellow brick, wood with stainless steel, and a bold selection of ceramic tiles fuse the space, filling it with interesting detail, but maintaining a feeling of open space.

Above A utility closet, on the left as you enter, has a double sink with shelving above and washing machine and dryer stacked on one side.

Far right The ceiling above the ground floor seating area creates an intimate retreat within the open-plan living space.

Right The ash-faced closet doors to ceiling level suggest height in the child's bedroom. A window seat disguises the slope of the roof.

Floor plans A triple-height unit has been converted for family living, retaining an open space that uses all of the available floor area at ground level. The staircase defines the hall, while a counter divides the kitchen from the living and dining area. The second floor houses a child's bedroom, a bathroom, and a galleried study. On the upper level the main bedroom is beneath a pitched roof. A circular bathroom sits behind the staircase top. The dressing room is on one side of the bathroom, and there is a closet on the other. Doors lead onto a terrace.

① **Hall** The front door opens onto the hall, which features plenty of storage space.

② **Living/dining area** The dining table occupies the double-height section. Light floods in from the open floor above and from two large windows and French doors in the wall at the front of the building. Seating is under the mezzanine.

③ **Utility closet and kitchen** On the left of the entrance is the utility closet, beside which is a kitchen space with room for a stove surrounded by floor and wall cabinets. The sink and dishwasher are in base cabinets; there is a refrigerator below the counter.

④ **Bedroom** The child's room has spacious built-in storage cupboards and plenty of floor space.

⑤ **Bathroom** A porthole window in this bathroom looks onto the hall.

⑥ **Study/home office** One of the owners is a student, so a work area was an essential space.

⑦ **Bedroom and bathroom** A walk-in dressing room/closet adjoining the bathroom means that a sleigh bed is all the furniture needed in the main bedroom.

⑧ **Terrace** Double doors lead out onto a wooden deck.

First floor

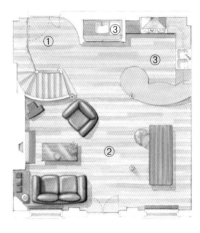

Second floor

Attic floor

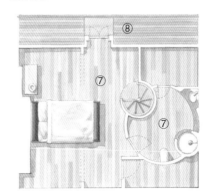

HOMEWORKING

In the last decade, developers have taken enthusiastically to converting unused industrial buildings for housing, and these transformations form the backbone of new residential property available in many urban areas. The Piper Building, decorated with mural panels by artist John Piper for British Gas in the early 1960s, is just such a development. For one young businessman, whose work involves a great deal of foreign travel, it offered the opportunity to mold from scratch a base in which he could live and work.

Architects Wells Mackereth were asked to design the 1,560-square-foot space. They removed the mezzanine that ran the full length of the apartment, since their client would be spending work and social time at home and they wanted to retain some double-height space to make the dwelling as airy as possible. A built-in kitchen wall was installed at one end, with overhead cabinets extending well above the height of conventional kitchen units. In the middle of the apartment is a spare bedroom bordered by two cross-storage walls on each side, the more central of which divides the living/working area from the sleeping/bathing area. The entrance hall stands on one side, with a narrow aisle running on the opposite side. Access to all the high storage cupboards and the mezzanine storage space over the foyer was achieved by installing a

Right The storage wall in the living/working space is designed to function on one side as an office, with desk, drawer, and shelf space; a sliding shutter door pulls down to conceal everything. On the left is the fireplace, plus recreational equipment – TV, VCR, stereo, and accompanying accessories – neatly stacked in boxes and drawers. On the left of the wall is the corridor leading to the bedroom and to the right is the foyer with mezzanine storage space above.

Left The architects designed this table for their client. An artfully engineered two-part structure, it has a black walnut veneered top and a metal gateleg support section on casters. Folded out, the table is spacious enough for meetings or to seat up to ten for dinner parties.

Main picture Custom-built in MDF and stainless steel, the built-in kitchen wall was painted a sharp shade of lilac to provide a colorful contrast to all the white and shades of gray. Floor-to-ceiling cabinets at one end are accessed by the portable, lightweight ladder.

Far right The home office desk and shelves are simply and quickly concealed by a sliding shutter that looks like a wall surface.

Right The foyer is under the mezzanine, and doubles as a closet, with hanging space for clothes and room below for boots and shoes. Boxes provide storage for bags, briefcases, and a fax machine, and help limit desk clutter.

continuous stainless-steel bar at a fixed height around the perimeter of the living/dining area and kitchen. A mezzanine was installed over the main bedroom: this holds the main bathroom (cleverly hidden from the bedroom) and a sleeping platform/storage space. Under the mezzanine are a walk-in dressing room/closet, a bathroom/utility room, and the entrance hall.

Ingenious detail abounds in the design of the fixtures throughout. Everything slides, glides, pushes, or pulls so that, when closed, the many cabinets and storage units appear to be wall space. Sliding shutters pull down to hide the desk; lightweight panels screen off windows; and a push-and-tilt panel conceals the TV. For someone who works from home and often holds business meetings there, the apartment presents a perfectly professional appearance, but everything is effortlessly and neatly tucked away out of sight once work is over.

Mezzanine

First floor

Floor plans The apartment was redesigned to include a mezzanine at the sleeping and bathing end, which left the living/dining area with the full double-height space.

① **Main bedroom** In one corner is a large walk-in closet with hanging space on one side and storage on the other.

② **Bathroom/utility room and foyer** These fit into the space beneath the mezzanine. Laundry equipment is kept out of sight in the bathroom/utility room.

③ **Spare bedroom** Full-height pivotal glass doors close off the spare bedroom from the main bedroom and living/dining area.

④ **Living/dining area** Slate gray sofas separate the kitchen/dining area from the multifunctional storage wall on the opposite side.

⑤ **Kitchen** Built-in cabinets hold the dishwasher and stove.

⑥ **Mezzanine** A galleried bathroom has a bathtub sunk into a raised dais on one end, and a shower on the other. On the other side of the divide is a sleeping platform/storage space.

LIVING

THE FRAMEWORK

The living room or den is where working people spend most of their time at home. In many households it has taken over from the kitchen as the hub and core of the home; it is a room of both activity and relaxation. For most of us, it is a place to retreat from the stresses and strains of the outside world, where you can curl up on the couch with a book or a magazine, lounge against a pile of pillows to watch television or listen to a new CD. It's where you sit and talk to your partner, children, or friends, and it should be somewhere you feel completely at ease. However, the living room is also likely to be the most public room in your home, a place where you entertain guests and endeavor to make them feel welcome and comfortable. And so it's the face or image that you present to the outside world – a statement of your personal style.

In addition to being somewhere to relax, in a small home, where the kitchen is not big enough to accommodate a table, the living room will double as a dining area, and the table may also be used for work or hobbies. Because it may be called upon to fulfill a variety of functions, the living room becomes a very complex room to organize and furnish. It is extraordinary, then, that whereas no one would even contemplate designing a bathroom or kitchen without drawing a scaled plan first, we have a much more haphazard approach to

Above A small one-story glassworks factory was converted by architects Hawkins Brown into a two-bedroom house with a study/guest room.

Right The living/dining area of the converted glassworks makes good use of the full height of the building. A wall and ceiling of glass maximize the openness so the room is flooded with natural light, whatever the weather outside. The sculptural staircase creates interesting shapes and corners in the room, with space for seating along one wall. Around the other side of the staircase, a neat square has been cut into the wall, which is used as a serving hatch between the kitchen and the dining area.

Left Designed to combine one- and two-story living, the main living area in this converted glassworks is beneath the lower end of a shallow sloping roof on the river side of the building. The smaller rooms and service areas – kitchen, bathrooms, bedrooms, and study – are neatly stacked on two levels at the front of the house overlooking the street. Angular roof space, clean architectural detail, and a wall of stairs with a galleried landing define the living area, while open doorways on both levels let light filter into the main space.

designing our living rooms. Not surprisingly, it makes good sense to get out the graph paper and plot the area, marking in permanent features such as the windows, doors, and fireplaces, and traffic flows to other rooms. In the living room, where electrical equipment is almost always essential, planning the location of outlets is important too. In addition to a television and video and audio equipment, it is also likely that various localized light sources will be needed for specific tasks, such as reading.

Once the fixed elements of the area have been drawn in, the key to making the living room work is getting the seating and storage elements right. If there is room, a good basis for seating is an arrangement of a couple of comfortable sofas – two-seaters are much more useful and ergonomic than single armchairs or three-seater sofas (people don't like sitting in rows in social situations). And try to provide half a dozen dining chairs that can double as occasional chairs when entertaining friends. Most of us watch some television in the living area, even if there are sets in other rooms, so the seating must be arranged to allow comfortable viewing. Seating also needs to facilitate conversation (we tend to turn our bodies toward people as we talk, and no one enjoys shouting across distances). Seats for solitary occupations, such as reading, also need to be considered.

One space-saving option in open-plan spaces is to store electrical equipment, accessories, and books on freestanding open shelving units that can also act as space dividers. In small rooms, even though the cost is likely to be considerably more, electrical equipment and the accompanying paraphernalia is usually more effectively stored when concealed on shelves and in drawers behind doors, along with the games, magazines, catalogs, and other bits and pieces that are part of our daily lives.

Keeping clutter behind closed doors wherever possible helps to maintain an overall impression of clean space, openness, and calm. If you want your home to appear larger than it is and to feel light and airy, a disciplined approach to storage is a top priority. Grouping those items chosen for display and limiting them to interesting arrangements in carefully selected areas will also help to maintain an uncluttered appearance.

It is difficult, however, to imagine a living area without any books or pictures. If you would find it impossible to live in a space without some personal belongings on view, then try to look for less obvious places to locate them. Install shelves to hold books or objets d'art high up on walls above doors or windows, and don't overlook the invaluable display space around and between windows.

ZONING WITH COLOR

Far left Architects Littman Goddard Hogarth used strong tones of orange and yellow to make a bold impact in a tiny studio. Used on moving screen doors and in small enclosed spaces, these colors are completely surrounded by a white ceiling and matching walls. With pale wood on all the floors, the space is not overwhelmed.

Left The bright orange door slides back to reveal the bedroom and conceal a translucent glass panel that lets borrowed light from the living area filter through into the internal bathroom. This not only opens up the bedroom area, it also provides more privacy in the bathroom. Checked orange and yellow bed-linen helps to establish a visual link between the different areas.

It is generally accepted that daytime rooms look best painted in pale, light tones to keep them as airy and spacious as possible. On the other hand, rooms that are used at night need bolder, richer colors, which are more responsive to the glow of electric light and have a warmer, more welcoming ambience. If your living area is small and is used in the day as well as in the evening, heavy colors on walls are not recommended since they would make it seem even smaller. But this does not mean that achieving an intimate and friendly atmosphere is ruled out altogether — it can still be accomplished with clever lighting. Nor should you outlaw strong color altogether in your home. Instead, think of using it in blocks, rather than across whole areas. Employing clean white tones or soothing neutral shades of cream, gray, or beige to decorate a basic shell means that even small areas of strong color will have a striking prominence. However, the overall impression of spaciousness will be maintained.

Just as you can use screens and walls of storage to divide areas within a room, so color can be used to delineate space. When these two devices are put together, they work very successfully. Particularly when an apartment contains only one main room, color can help to visually partition areas set aside for different functions —

Right To make the most
of a sloping glass roof
on one side and an open
balcony terrace on the
other, architects Ash
Sakula placed the living
room in a tiny house on
the top floor. Views
across the urban skyline
enhance the volume of
space in the room.
Painted white, the strong
angular fireplace and
dramatic curve at the top
of the staircase create a
form of structural pattern
that enhances the
framework of the room.
The boldly colored
furnishings act as focal
points.

for example, the working corner, the cooking/eating space, and the area for sleeping or watching television. To achieve different zones in a room, you don't need to restrict color to large blocks of vertical space, such as screens, walls, or closets. The upholstery fabrics chosen for sofas and seating units can trigger the same visual effect and make a seating area appear slightly separate from the rest of the room.

Quite often, monochromatic schemes are still the first choice in small spaces, but without using strong variations in color, it is still possible to achieve a similar, but more subtle, effect by using texture to add visual depth and to mark out functional territory. Grainy wooden floorboards, chalky flat-finish paintwork, crisp smooth linen, and knobby woolen bouclé are all rich, natural textures that make an interesting contrast to the more raw surfaces of concrete, stone, stainless steel, and shiny, reflective paint.

The use of pattern in small spaces needs to be rationed. Pattern tends to demand most of the attention in a room and eats up visual space quite greedily. Instead of introducing pattern through wall finishes, textiles, or carpets, consider collections of small, contained accessories, such as groups of black-and-white photographs, a shelf of books, or even a single row of identical drinking glasses.

Right A small apartment above commercial premises was converted by architects Granit, who removed the ceiling and pitched a glazed roof behind the existing parapet. This created a greater sense of space and light in the main living area, and meant a mezzanine level for a bedroom and bathroom could be added.

Below The open design of the new wooden staircase allows light to flood in from the glass roof down the stairway to the entrance door. The reinforced front wall is used extensively for storage (bookshelves also act as an extra sound and insulation barrier).

CREATING SPACE
Improving the spatial quality of your living area is about illusion: making the space appear much larger than it really is. This effect can be achieved in a variety of ways, although they are grouped here in three quite different categories: redecoration, reorganization, and lighting. Redecoration is the most basic and easily achieved technique, as well as the least expensive. It can lighten and brighten up a room, making it appear more spacious.

Improving the organization of a room so there is a place for everything can bring a clean, uncluttered visual order and efficiency to the room, making it calming to live with. It helps enormously when you are creating a living area to take an imaginative approach – for example, by planning ways to incorporate storage into the fabric and framework of a room, instead of introducing extra items of furniture.

If this is not an option, when buying furniture look for pieces with dual-purpose potential. Trunks and chests double as storage spaces or low tables to hold magazines and coffee cups, and if you place a cushion on top, they can even be used as occasional seats. In properties where the windows project out, the classic approach to make optimum use of the space is to build a low cupboard with a seat cushion on top. Today, an enormous selection of sofas and daybeds – for sitting and sleeping – is available, as well as

Below The owner of this apartment has a large collection of CDs to house. Storage space was designed to fit unobtrusively below the wooden ledge on top of the staircase wall, where it would still be easily accessible.

upholstered footstools with bed mechanisms folded inside. Smaller items, such as stools that convert into stepladders to access high storage space, are also worth investigating.

Structural changes require more commitment, both financially and imaginatively. However, sometimes small and relatively straight-forward changes, such as removing a partition wall to open up internal views and reshape the living area, result in the most startling improvements. Where a generous amount of ceiling height is available, the addition of a gallery or mezzanine offers an exciting and dramatic change. It can alter the volume of space, as well as increasing the floor area, to provide at least one other useful "room" that could be designated as, say, a home office.

At the top of many buildings, roof space offers an equally dramatic and wide choice of spatial options. If the area is opened up by removing the ceiling, adding skylights, or even a glass roof, the space can be transformed to become inspiringly alive and light-filled. In a city, a panoramic view over an eclectic collection of rooftops can have a dramatic appeal to rival the softness of a country landscape.

Few of us have the confidence (or the essential building knowledge) to make structural alterations without professional help. While simple, internal partition walls or basic gallery structures may

Left Fashion designer Ben de Lisi discussed storage ideas for his London apartment with his interior designer, Adam Dolle, during the initial stages of planning. Dolle suggested building cavity walls in the living room, ostensibly to create interest and shape in what was a plain, square room lacking any architectural features, but also to hide utility pipes and wiring, and to allow shelving for books and magazines to be neatly recessed into the walls.

Right In de Lisi's apartment, a freestanding wall, built in American walnut, serves to separate the living room from the tiny kitchen beyond. It was designed to allow light from the kitchen windows to flood the entire space. The room is furnished with classic sculptural shapes that are contained and precise, leaving clean, open space all around them.

not need planning permission, it is likely that an extension or attic remodel will require some form of official approval, and there may also be fire regulations to comply with. If in doubt, always seek advice first (*see* pp.124–5).

In houses and apartments where structural change is not an option, and the living area has limitations – a low ceiling, for example – opening up the room in an attempt to make it airy and spacious may not be the right answer. A helpful alternative is to break up the space with a screen or dividing panel that does not reach the full height of the room. A screen lets you define boundaries without building doors. By sectioning off an area – for eating or cooking, say – with a partition that allows light to filter over and through from above, and positioning the screened-off area at the farthest point from entry into the room, the space is given a focal point. Screening also gives the impression that there is a similar volume of space on the other side of the partition.

Partitions can be inexpensive tools for dividing up space. They may be used either to section off an area for a specific function, or to hide things away in lieu of cupboards. Partitions can be made from panels of particleboard or plywood, hinged together and given a coat of paint; this is within the abilities of even the most unenthusiastic

Left Architects AEM increased the volume of usable space in this apartment by removing the ceiling and roof trusses, and supporting the roof pitches on new steelwork. On the right of the stairs is the bathroom and a small office/storage room/spare bedroom. At the top is a bed platform. Beyond the stairs and kitchen cabinets lies the dining space and a seating area.

Right The main living area in the same tiny apartment is divided and defined by the angular shape of a hit-or-miss staircase. Doors were added to the shapes, and spaces created by the treads on one side of the stairs turn into useful storage space. On the other side of the stairs, kitchen cabinets fit neatly under the framework.

handyperson. Although sandblasted glass, set into full-height frames anchored to floor and ceiling, needs to be put in by an experienced installer, it is another excellent way of creating a visual barrier. The real advantage in this case is that borrowed light filters through the whole area of the screen from the space beyond.

If you plan the lighting at the same time as the layout of the room, it is easier to achieve the right balance between privacy and spaciousness in a multifunctional living space. A general level of background, ambient lighting supplied from recessed ceiling lights or track lights will illuminate corners of the room without making shadows and will create an illusion of greater space. This form of lighting is all that is necessary for moving around the room, having conversations, and watching television. Writing, reading, and working at a computer all require localized task lighting, which is more easily supplied by table, desk, and floor lamps. It also makes sense to invest in dimmer switches to provide maximum flexibility and control of light, allowing subtle mood changes in a room, from cool brightness to a soft warm glow (dimmer switches can be wired to overhead fixtures and to the electrical circuit for lamps).

Right The ultimate in
discretion, this television
is sleekly unobtrusive,
recessed into the wall
space, with all of its
unattractive workings and
wiring concealed at the
back.

COOKING & EATING

THE FRAMEWORK

Above all, a kitchen is a functional room, primarily a place where meals are prepared and cooked. For many of us, though, food is much more than just a source of energy, and cooking is an enjoyable part of everyday life, rather than a tedious chore. If you spend much time in the kitchen, efficiency, style, comfort, and ambience will all be very important considerations.

At the other end of the scale, if you seldom cook or eat at home, creating a conventional style of kitchen will be a waste of time and money. This also applies when space is at a premium. In this case, a better solution is to organize a neat little counter area to accommodate necessities — a sink, stove, refrigerator, and maybe a microwave oven — that can be tucked away behind a screen in the corner of your living area, or possibly behind a door in a hall or corridor.

If kitchens are required to operate on a higher culinary level than simply warming up a croissant or pouring water into the coffeemaker, a little more thought is necessary. The basic plan in all kitchens, whatever their size, is that the three essentials — sink, cooking facilities, and refrigerator — need to be within about a double arm's-span reach of each other to form a working triangle. Counter and

Left Storage units on casters are incredibly versatile. In this tiny attic kitchen, the units pull out for easy access to the contents and give extra counter space. They can be wheeled to different areas and slide neatly away after use. Here, every inch of vertical space is utilized for storage, with a rack for wine bottles suspended from the eaves and a metal bar to hold utensils fitted under the window frame.

Above Wooden storage units form a jigsaw puzzle of shapes, which use every bit of wall space and look good open or closed. Pantry units are behind the center panels with appliances on each side.

Below A central cube-shaped dining "room" was designed by architects Littman Goddard & Hogarth to fit in the middle of the main living area. A table folds away to resemble a sculpture.

Below right The hinged tabletop unclips from its wall slot and can be opened out to half-size.

Right When extended, there is room for six at the table, and use is made of the corridor and overflow from the kitchen space. The chairs are easily stacked when not in use.

storage space are positioned between the triangle points, providing a choice of surfaces to prepare and put things on, and cabinets, drawers, shelves, racks, and so on to store ingredients and hold cooking pots, pans, and utensils. This is the basis of a kitchen.

Before you venture out to choose cabinets and equipment, it makes sense to examine how you live and what you really need, and to design your kitchen accordingly. For someone who works all day, has no time to shop for anything other than essentials during the week, and cooks most evenings for one or two people at the most, good storage facilities for food, including a spacious refrigerator, freezer, and pantry, are main priorities. People who love to cook and

entertain, have friends dropping in for meals on a regular (if casual) basis, and are able to shop often have different requirements. They need more work space, plus plenty of storage room for pots, pans, and serving and eating dishes, as well as adequate storage space for food. These people probably feel happier with a friend or two to chat with them in the kitchen, avoiding the sense of cooking in isolation while everyone else is enjoying pre-dinner drinks. If the kitchen has room for a table and chairs, this is not a problem (it is convenient, where possible, to have a dining area in the kitchen in any event, since with the demise of the formal dining space, eating takes place in the kitchen much of the time anyway).

With the opportunity to start from scratch, you may decide on an open-plan kitchen design, combining cooking/eating/living space, or you may want to allocate a separate living area so the kitchen only needs to be large enough for eating and entertaining. If there is just enough room for essentials and big structural changes are not an option, look at ways of opening up the kitchen to the living area. If the kitchen leads off a corridor, would double doors (or no door at all) make the room appear more accessible and less isolated? Alternatively (and an idea that seems to be in vogue again), is it possible to install a serving hatch?

STORAGE

A run of unbroken kitchen cabinets, with no intrusive knobs or dials, has a clean, streamlined appearance. Everything is hidden away and in its place, so the overall effect is one of spaciousness. In the kitchen, built-in units have even more validity than in other areas of the home; they can even conceal all your major appliances. Today's manufacturers produce furniture containing every type of drawer, basket, shelf, and rack to pull, slide, or fold out and hold any piece of equipment, food package, or jar that you are ever likely to own. There is something very calming about having a place for everything and everything in its place. Tiny kitchens, however, especially the classic galley shape where counters run along parallel walls, or U-shaped kitchens where three walls are utilized, are not suited to banks of built-in cabinets because the framework and doors take up too much space. There is also the argument that built-in cabinets seem clinical and cold.

Ask yourself, then, do you want to have everything hidden away? If you eat and entertain in the kitchen, the atmosphere should be welcoming. After all, the kitchen is a place where the senses very much come alive. Smell, touch, taste, and sight all have their role to play in the preparing, cooking, and serving of food. A pile of terracotta bowls brought home from a Latin American vacation, wooden

Above On a raised dais in the corner of the main living area of this two-story apartment, designed by Circus Architects, built-in wall and base cabinets are defined by bright red doors. A dwarf wall with a black granite counter combines with the raised level and color zoning to visually separate this area.

Right When the cabinet doors are closed, this kitchen wall appears as a block of strong vital color with a stainless-steel box in the center. A selection of cooking appliances, including a microwave in the space directly above the main oven, are all neatly hidden away behind the doors to give a stylish, uncluttered feeling.

spoons in a basket bought at a street market, well-worn bread boards discovered in thrift stores, and racks holding *batterie de cuisine* assembled over the years are all evocative objects that you may not wish to hide away. On the other hand, despite their charm, unstructured kitchens have few labor-saving qualities and would probably irritate a busy person living in a small space. A compromise, retaining an unstructured or semi-unstructured look without losing the built-in organization of a modern kitchen, may be just what is needed.

Floor-standing units, installed along the kitchen walls to hold appliances, gadgets, equipment, some food storage, and the sink, will give you all the efficiency you need. Open shelves and racks above work surfaces allow you to stack items that you find attractive, but also use regularly, so there is no time for dust to gather. Here, you can introduce color and style. Display rustic plates and bowls in rich, vivid shades of ocher, jade green, and indigo blue, or a row of plain, elegant white plates or pitchers beside a stack of stainless-steel saucepans, a stoneware mortar and pestle, or a line of cookbooks. It makes sense, and saves time and effort, too, to have useful equipment and utensils ready at hand and visible, yet stored above work-surface level so preparation space does not become cluttered.

Left This ground-floor kitchen fits under a sloping wall created by a staircase. Originally one long narrow room, dining and cooking areas are now separated by a dividing wall. A large square doorway and tall open window slots allow natural light into the room from the dining space beyond. The built-in area is contained beneath a beech counter, and white appliances sit alongside white-painted cupboard doors. A large collection of stainless-steel pots and pans and a rail of utensils, gathered together over the years, are all accessible and a pleasure to look at.

Below A collection of much-loved china, glass, and silver adds rich warmth when grouped in glass-fronted shelves on the wall at the dining end of the kitchen.

ZONING WITH COLOR

However much we enjoy cooking, few of us regard the kitchen as a place where we can totally relax. It's an active, doing type of room, albeit active and doing at different speeds. At the beginning of the day we want it to be a bright, breezy, upbeat place, challenging the brain to wake up as we make the coffee, squeeze the oranges for juice, toast the bread, and digest the daily news. Preparing an evening meal still calls for a clean, efficient, working environment, but with more mood and ambience. At this time of day a glass of wine and a plate of olives is set on the counter beside you to be savored as you cook the *tagliatelle*, toss the salad, and discuss the day with your partner or friends.

White is the color that represents clean efficiency, and, as in all small rooms, decorating with white enhances the feeling of spaciousness. The kitchen interiors illustrated in this book reflect the current vogue of relying on white to create an illusion of space by using it all over the framework, walls, ceiling, baseboards, window frames, and so on. Blocks of bright color are then introduced on cabinet doors and other furniture. Tuscan burnt orange, bright acid yellow, and deep indigo blue feature widely, as do red and black, the traditional lacquer colors. These are all sharp, bold, confident colors that can hold their own against each other, as well as against the

Right The owners of this apartment decided on bright lacquer colors, red and black, to create a bold, upbeat statement in this minute kitchen/dining room. Designed by the architects Granit, a curved work bar juts out from the wall to form the main work surface and hold the stove. The space underneath contains the oven, dishes, and saucepans. Every inch of vertical space is equipped with shelves, racks, and hooks for storage.

Far right Closets on each side of the window are painted red to draw them into the color scheme. The closets, which hold the TV and other everyday items, are deep enough to give space for a window seat. On the near wall, open shelves hold interesting objects to shift attention from the radiator below. The checked floor and red-painted areas make this room appear very colorful; the majority of the space is, in fact, white.

strong, angular shapes and upbeat surroundings of contemporary kitchens. Color defines and delineates space, and in this room, where the activities of cooking and eating may often take place simultaneously, contrasting hues can help to separate the cooking/working zone from the eating/relaxing zone. Boldly colored floor cabinets with open shelving above are less obtrusive than matching wall-mounted cabinets because the strong color is below eye level, but it still balances out the accessories above the work surface.

An interesting development in kitchen design is the practice of combining contemporary hardwearing materials, such as stainless steel and brushed aluminum, with their traditional, solid counterparts of stone, granite, slate, and marble. All of these materials make excellent surfaces that will withstand the daily round of water, grease, and sharp knives. Their naturally handsome appearance changes to take on the character of whatever they are teamed with, be it intense bursts of chic, jazzy color or cool and classic light-colored wood. Using different materials for countertops and backsplashes helps to separate different areas used for different purposes. Stainless steel, marble, and granite are good for surfaces that will be splashed with water and oils; sealed, waxed, or stained wood is suitable everywhere else in the cooking/eating area.

CREATING SPACE Once you have decided

on the framework (wholly or partially built-in) and the color scheme
(pale shades, or all-white, for example), the kitchen can be further
streamlined by the efficient organization of storage. However, before
you try to find the right storage fixtures, study your kitchen
paraphernalia. Be ruthless and get rid of gadgets, dishes, and

anything else that is never used. Figure out what you really need. Are different sets of china and glass important, or would you be happy with a design that you can replace, when necessary? Dishes should be just as versatile as dual-purpose furniture. Look for bowls that work equally well for desserts and salads, and freezer- or ovenproof dishes that can go directly to the table.

Storage units that slide out on tracks tend to be more useful in tight spaces – pulled out, you can see exactly what you have. They can be equipped with baskets, trays, and shelves to hold everything from cereal boxes to saucepans. Units on casters can be pulled around for easy access, and they can be moved to different parts of the kitchen as needed. If you are stuck with conventional cabinets, customize them to suit your needs – for example, by removing the central shelves and replacing them with sets of baskets on runners. Keep work surfaces clear, but hang a rod at backsplash height for utensils. If you can sacrifice some counter depth, have wall cabinets that come down to meet it to hold bulky items that are awkward to haul up from floor units (if possible, create work surfaces to slide out from under the original spaces). Consider appliances in compact or slimline versions, and small ovens that can be built into wall or base cabinets.

Far left Separate eating areas are not usually an option in small homes. In this kitchen, just enough space to hold a table and chairs has been created. Visual space and light is "borrowed" from the open corridor beyond.

Left A tall, thin room converted into a kitchen, with one wall devoted to cooking/storage space, economically utilizes a high vertical wall area. Natural light pours in over the work surface and sink.

Above The main living area has been divided by a half-glazed wall to create a separate space for cooking. Kitchen and built-in seating units around the table are pushed into the corners to use up all the space.

Above The combination of stainless-steel saucepans, skillets, and colanders on wooden shelves is both attractive and practical. Fluorescent lights installed under lower shelves illuminate the countertops below.

DISPLAY IDEAS

Kitchen paraphernalia looks wonderful on display – when it is done thoughtfully. Items with real character, such as glass mason jars filled with brown sugar, plump raisins, or colorful varieties of pasta, look attractive and wholesome when set together in neat, straight rows. Ceramic mixing bowls – stacked Leaning Tower of Pisa–fashion, have an equally appealing, random charm of their own. However, discrimination is an important watchword when you decide exactly what to put on open shelves – half-used tubes of tomato paste and open bags of flour just don't have quite the same aesthetic quality. Fill open shelves immediately above counters with attractive items that are used regularly (but make sure that food is not placed directly above steamy areas, such as sinks and stoves).

Alternatively, a not-quite-so-accessible shelf directly above a window or a door could be used to hold a special collection of pitchers or platters that are used only occasionally. Window space used for shelves generally goes against the principle (and natural instinct) of allowing as much light into a room as possible. When space is at a premium, though, and the view is less than good, a row of shiny saucepans outlined against the sky can be worth the compromise. Open-grid metal racks are great forms of shelving.

Left Shutting out natural light is normally anathema to architects. In this situation, however, where storage space is extremely tight, the view uninspiring, and another source of natural light is available, open shelves have been installed. They help to give a sense of balance to the long run of floor-standing kitchen cabinets underneath and distract attention from the fact that the two windows are not the same size.

Easy to install, they have a contemporary, industrial appeal that works well with a minimalist or classical style of decorating. In addition, they have the advantage of allowing the light to come through, which is especially important when they are positioned over work space. Hanging racks are equally good. When suspended from the ceiling and made from different types of metal and wood (or combinations of the two), they make use of the vertical space directly above your head and turn storage into a versatile, changeable art form. Open metal baskets, full of colorful vegetables such as peppers, and hooks holding strings of garlic, bundles of fragrant herbs, and garlands of red chiles suspended in the air alongside metal beaters, strainers, and cooking pans, turn a workroom into a proper kitchen and make good use of otherwise wasted space.

Other forms of storage, such as metal or wooden plate racks, also work well as practical, yet decorative, display devices. A plate rack above the sink removes the need for a draining board. When the rack is built above a stove, plates and serving dishes are kept warm and accessible. Shaker-style peg rails work in the same way when used to display *batterie de cuisine*, so that often-used equipment is readily accessible and also forms an interesting decorative focus.

Left Open metal shelving above the stainless-steel counter in this kitchen is designed so items can be stacked on top, slotted into place, or hung from it. Once washed, plates and glasses can be left to drain there to avoid countertop clutter.

Top If you need to use window space for shelving, the open metal variety has the advantage of letting as much light through as possible.

Bottom An old storage shelf, painted the same color as the walls, holds a treasured collection of *batterie de cuisine*, with strings of chiles and garlic conveniently positioned on the wall next to the stove. A metallic knife holder fits into the space below.

SLEEPING

THE FRAMEWORK

For some people the bedroom is a peaceful haven, a calm retreat, and a place of sanctuary at the end of the day. For others it is a waste of valuable space. Certainly, when space is at a premium, devoting a large chunk of it to an area unused during daylight hours might seem recklessly indulgent. On the positive side, bedrooms can often take up "awkward" space that is difficult and impractical to use for purposes other than sleeping. The eaves in attic rooms are a good example, having traditionally served as interesting and neat spaces for the horizontal attributes of the bed. Rooms with limited access to natural light – those facing into the well of an apartment building, basements, and even ground-floor rooms looking onto city streets – are ideal for bedrooms. As long as you can live without feeling the sun on your face when you wake up, and can bear having the bedroom below, rather than above, the place where you live, cook, and eat, these rooms can be the perfect choice.

In many small homes a bedroom needs to play a dual-purpose role. It might have to double as a study or an office if you work from home. The bedroom might even be part of the main living area in a small apartment or, in a family home, an alternative space for listening to music, watching television, or using a computer. In these instances,

Above In this apartment designed by Littman Goddard Hogarth, a small room off the living area serves as both a spare bedroom and an office. A panel, painted the same color as the wall, has been added to the bottom of a folding double bed to screen it from sight when not in use.

Center At the head of the bed a hinge mechanism makes pulling the bed out a simple operation. Straps span the mattress to hold bedding in place.

Right When it has been pulled down, the bed is just as comfortable as a conventional version. Recessed into the closet, which provides a convenient side table, the head of the bed is comfortably enclosed. A sliding etched glass door on the far side provides privacy but lets light through.

where having a bed in full view isn't conducive to the other activities that take place in the room, there are various options. Beds that fold down from the wall are space-saving and convenient: the bed effectively "disappears," folding away complete with bedding, and can be disguised to become simply part of the wall. It can be neatly hidden away behind various types of screens, such as sliding doors or venetian blinds; and storage facilities – shelves, cupboards, drawers, and hanging space – can be arranged around the bed area to make use of the whole wall. The main advantage of this type of bed, as opposed to a sofa bed or a futon, is that it can be quickly put away in the morning and pulled out at night – completely made up and ready to use. Another plus is that the floor space occupied for sleeping can be used for other purposes once the bed is put away. Any furniture used in that floor space should be lightweight and easy to move, or on casters, so it does not become an obstacle late at night when you are tired, or in the morning when you are in a hurry.

Another option is a sleeping platform, bed deck, or gallery, where the bed does not completely disappear from view, but is moved up onto a higher plane. Adding another level to a room in this way is aesthetically pleasing and makes a wonderfully dramatic impact, whether the style is minimalist, contemporary, or traditionally grand.

Where ceiling heights are generous and there is room for a large mezzanine or gallery, there will be space below to create an enclosed room, such as a bathroom, or an open seating area that would be lent a sense of comfort and intimacy by the lower ceiling. Even in rooms where the ceilings are not so lofty, there may be enough room to create an agreeably snug sleeping platform with plenty of space for bookshelves or cupboards underneath.

Major structural changes – a new mezzanine level, for example – require professional advice. On the other hand, a bed platform with storage below may be achieved with your own design input and the help of a capable carpenter (always check that the floor can bear the load first). Stairs providing access to the bed may be just as visually theatrical as the platform itself, and can play an exciting sculptural role in the dynamics of a room, especially in open-plan spaces. Spiral staircases are a prime example, and they use up only a small amount of floor space in comparison with conventional staircases.

Whether your bed is on a platform in an open-plan area or in a room of its own, it is clearly the main consideration when furnishing a bedroom, closely followed by storage requirements. Single beds are easy to plan around: they look neat and angular up against walls or centered under windows. Double or king-size beds, on the other

Left A lower ground-floor bedroom borrows light from other areas through etched-glass wall panels. Solid color separates the staircase from the bedroom and forms a sculptural screen between bed and door.

Above In a tiny bedroom, the bed sits against the low wall space under a dormer window, with storage below accessible via side and end panels. The bed linen provides a bold block of color in an otherwise neutral shell.

hand, are more likely to take up most of the floor space in small bedrooms and become the main focal point. As the majority of time spent in a bedroom is likely to be taken up in using the bed, shortage of space shouldn't necessarily be a problem. In fact, it may even enhance the feeling of comfort and intimacy. Once you have come to terms with the fact that your bed may fill the room, you could just go with the idea and opt for something that will dwarf the room, but express your personal style – a splendid antique bed in carved mahogany or polished brass, for example, or the simple, bold, structural good looks of a modern four-poster bed.

Bedroom storage – the other essential – has to be carefully planned (the potential for messiness in this room is considerable, and clutter makes small spaces seem even smaller). Clothes, shoes, and accessories all need to be hung and stacked so they can be stored and retrieved easily. Built-in closets that hide everything neatly away behind closed doors that slide, rather than open out, are the best option in very confined areas, leaving clean space after the bed has taken pride of place. And if there is no room for even this type of storage, consider the argument that dressing in a bedroom is a convention, rather than a necessity: it might make sense to put up hanging space elsewhere in your home.

Far left In the stylish and contemporary bedroom of a city apartment, Circus Architects has designed a low-level bed that seems to float above the floor. Low-level shelving on each side of the bed (more storage is provided in the adjoining dressing room and bathroom areas) and clean white walls and bed linens pull the eye toward the focal point: the fabulous skyline beyond the window.

Left Structural pillars act as both a full-height headboard and the framework for an opening etched-glass panel. Controlled by hydropneumatic gas springs, it opens over the double-height living area, adding to the spectacular view from the bedroom. When closed, the glass lets borrowed light filter through from the space beyond.

CREATING SPACE

The very fact that a bed takes up so much space can be used to advantage, if you utilize the areas around and beneath it properly. Studio-bed bases with storage facilities are widely available; storage is usually in the form of shallow drawers that slide out and is suitable mainly for folded clothes or bed linen. If space is really confined and you need to make use of the whole drawer, measure how far it extends and check that other furniture in the room will not impede access.

A platform built under a mattress may inspire you to create custom-made storage to suit your requirements. You could use boxes with racks inside for storing shoes, shelves for piles of shirts, and drawers for underwear and accessories. Spaces at the head and foot of a bed can also be useful storage areas. Instead of using bedside tables to hold a lamp, book, and glass of water, choose an item that doubles as storage, such as a chest of drawers or a small trunk.

Another option is to make a headboard with a shelf area on top that extends beyond the width of the bed, while wall-mounted furniture, lighting, or shelving – which still allows you to see the area underneath – creates the illusion of space. Mirrors, when applied to all or part of a wall or to closet doors, work cleverly both to visually extend space and to amplify the light.

Left An attic master bedroom in a three-story apartment is accessed from a spiral staircase. The curved line is repeated at the top of the stairs and in the curved wall surrounding a circular shower room underneath the roof pitch. A closet below the sloping roof is angled to blend in with the shape.

Below The full width of the bedroom is kept by running oak floorboards into the apexes where floor and roof meet. The headboard wall extends out on each side to hold reading lights. A sleigh-bed is the only piece of furniture taking up the valuable floor space.

ZONING WITH COLOR

For some of us the bedroom is about relaxation: the atmosphere needs to be soft, sensual, and gently tranquil. Others require a bright, crisply clean "wake-up" look. Whatever your temperament, there are a couple of points to consider before making a decision. For most of us, the bedroom is used in the bright natural light of morning and the soft artificial light of evening – you'll want to study your chosen color at both ends of the day. Certain colors, such as green and yellow, can change character quite considerably in warm artificial light. Fashionable orange, for example, can overheat and be uncomfortably strong in a small space. If you want to make the room appear as spacious as possible, use white, neutrals, or shades of the same pale to midtone color (mix varying quantities of white with the darkest tone chosen) on all surfaces. Walls, flooring, curtains or blinds, bed linens, and features such as radiators, all colored in the same or similar tones, create fewer of the visual breakpoints that can disrupt a room.

Alternatively, if you wish to make a feature out of the intimacy of the space, dark, jewel-like colors will intensify the atmosphere. Remember, too, that color can draw attention to a particular area, enliven a room devoid of architectural features, or simply distract from an unattractive view.

Right Fashion designer Ben de Lisi has effectively color-zoned his tiny bedroom and bathroom space using rich, earthy tones of neutral colors with white and black. White lifts the ceiling and, combined with a black-and-glass screen wall, it separates the bathing area from the bedroom.

Far right A mirrored wall reflects light from the ceiling, and the putty-colored carpet on the floor exaggerates the impression of space. From this angle, custom-built storage cubes take on a double dimension, too. The headboard has floor-to-ceiling closets on each side, plus a place to mount bedside wall lights and recessed, neat shelving space.

DISPLAY IDEAS

For those who truly are meticulously neat, bedroom storage affords the opportunity to play with interesting forms of display. The neat symmetry of jackets, slacks, skirts, and dresses hanging in a line, shelves stacked with piles of crisply pressed shirts, and rows of shoes in the space beneath create a whole wall of pattern and color in a room. You can also try clustering other elements that you wish to display to create a stronger impact. Books, paintings, photograph frames, and collections of smaller items all make bolder statements when grouped together, providing a room with a focal point. Objects displayed in open shelving, with mirrors on the wall behind, will seem more defined and distinct.

Instead of using up floor space, use walls and, in particular, higher spaces for decorative storage. The tops of cabinets are excellent places to display larger items and sculpturally strong shapes such as vases, jars, old leather suitcases, and interesting boxes, including those of the circular hat variety (which also make useful storage). Narrow shelves built at above-shoulder or head height, again displaying sculptural or simple circular shapes, lift the level of focus and extend the height of the room. The key to exaggerating space is to keep the room clean and uncluttered; if this is not in your nature, it's better to admit it and hide everything away.

Left Not intimidated by lack of space in this small bedroom, the owner has used a framework of neutral tones and white to create a spacious setting and filled it with large pieces of furniture and eye-catching features. An imposing marble fireplace, which has been decorated with paintings and candlesticks, creates a strong focal point.

Below left A cluster of photograph frames draws the eye to the window and the light and space beyond. The depth of the windowsill is extended by shelf space created from a boxed-in radiator. A large abstract oil painting in the corridor leading to the bedroom is paler in tone than the wall below, making the area appear taller.

BATHING

THE FRAMEWORK

When it comes to the bathroom, it is generally accepted that space is restricted. This room is often considered almost as an afterthought and frequently gets squeezed into a windowless area too small for any other use. However, bathroom layouts need to be carefully planned, not just to make sure that everything fits in, but also to allow comfortable access to fixtures. To help you with this, manufacturers of bathroom furniture often supply catalogs with printed grids and cutout shapes to represent the fixtures. The least expensive and simplest option is to place fixtures as close to the relevant water supply or drain line as possible. However, saving money on pipework can be a false economy if it means more alterations later on.

Bathroom designers often complain that traditional pedestal fixtures, which are floor-anchored, waste space. Wall-hung versions make small bathrooms seem larger, and they can be hung at the height to suit you. Wall-mounted faucets can be space savers, too.

Where space is restricted, a quirky color scheme, which might overwhelm a larger room, is an idea; using slightly more expensive materials may also be a possibility. Whatever your bathroom size, surfaces should be water resistant, but don't let this inhibit your choice of style.

Far left White ceramic tiles, clean and fresh, are a practical, space-enhancing choice. The wall-mounted sink is semi-inset into a tiled shelf that extends under the opaque glass block window, keeping the line of the wall unobtrusive.

Left The tank and all the pipework for this toilet have been neatly boxed in. False paneling, with a useful shelf on top, is covered in the same tiles as the wall. Pale monochromatic color schemes always help to give a spacious feel to a room.

Right This shower room and toilet cubicle designed by Wells Mackereth manifests clean space in every sense. Recessed sections hold toilet paper on one side of the room and a mirror on the other. Fixtures to operate the shower and toilet are also recessed, as are the light fixtures that illuminate the area. Sliding etched-glass doors allow light to filter through, and a network of putty-colored mosaic tiles makes the room appear sleek and stylish.

Below This shower room has one wall of stationary glass panels and another with sliding doors, providing easy access and lots of light. Aquamarine mosaics create a watery mood; recessed fixtures give a streamlined look.

Below This shower room has one wall of stationary glass panels and another with sliding doors, providing easy access and lots of light. Aquamarine mosaics create a watery mood; recessed fixtures give a streamlined look.

Right In a bathroom that receives natural light, glass bricks were used for the walls and a shower cubicle. Large areas of mirror and cream mosaic tiles help to maintain the sense of space and light in this room.

SHOWERS

Exhilarating and energizing, the shower does more than simply cleanse. If there's no room for a bathtub at all, a shower can always be created by lining the walls of a room with tiles and installing a drainage hole in the floor. Alternatively, low-profile shower bases with drainage holes can be partly recessed into the floor. When positioned behind etched-glass or glass-brick screens, they are less claustrophobic because of the filtered light (and screens, of course, protect the other fixtures from the water). Heating pipes set under the floor tiles will keep the shower warm and dry.

If you have space for an enclosed shower, you can design your own screening doors. Glass (the toughened safety variety) is the obvious material; alternatively, think about etched-glass or glass-brick panels. If your shower is a tiled alcove, the "door" can simply be a shower curtain on a rod. Shower doors, available hinged or pivoting, can be reversed to hang on either side. Sliding doors, consisting of two or more panels that overlap when opened, are space savers, and accordion-style sliding doors are another option. Shower bases are made of acrylic or molded fiberglass in a choice of sizes, shapes, and colors. Corner versions are designed in a triangular shape to fit into the space (shower enclosure doors and panels are available to fit around them).

BATHTUBS

For some people a shower's stimulating effects will never replace the soothing ritual of bathing, and they will go to great lengths to install a bathtub in the smallest of bathrooms. Of course, it has always been possible to position shower heads and fixtures at one end for a dual-purpose bath (shower heads on faucets are useful for washing hair but not the same as "real" showers), but today there are tubs specially designed for showering. These have a wider section at the "shower end" of the bathtub, and the end wall panel runs straight down, rather than sloping, to meet the bottom of the tub at a right angle. In a small bathroom where there is not enough space for a separate shower and bathtub, this is probably the best compromise.

Shower screens that extend the whole length of the tub are available to help contain splashing. A standard bathtub is about 2 x 5 feet and maintains a full width from end to end (though a larger size offers more generous maneuvering space). Most bathroom furniture manufacturers produce bathtubs in several different sizes, which can be as small as 3 feet square. However, unless it is fairly deep, such a tub would be very unsatisfactory to use (water lapping just above waist height is a novelty in a hotel, but at the end of a working day it would inevitably be a disappointment).

Far left In this minuscule bathroom the architects have managed to create enough space for a tub, which slots neatly into a closet-sized space. Faucets are recessed into the tiled wall on one side, and the window above the marble shelf faces onto the lightwell of the building.

Left Another "illusion" may be achieved by sinking a tub into the floor or a platform. In this bathroom mezzanine, the bathtub has been sunk into a stepped dais so it effectively disappears. Beneath the balustrade, a walnut bench seat lifts up to reveal storage space for towels, toilet paper, and so on.

Above Pipework is concealed behind painted wooden panels. Faucets and a water spout are mounted on the wall above the inset bowl to leave the surrounding area free. Directly below the bowl is useful storage space.

SINKS

Bathroom sinks come in many shapes and sizes, but in a small room, where a pedestal will simply use up valuable floor space and create unhygienic nooks and crannies, a sink that cantilevers off the wall is a better option. Very small versions, designed for use in half-baths, tuck into corners or recess into walls, but are only really suitable for washing hands. However, there are good-sized sinks designed for corner spaces, with openings at the back for standard faucets. Innovative creations can be purchased from designers such as Philippe Starck, who has produced sinks with modest outer dimensions and generous "counter" space to hold toiletries, makeup, and so on. Wall-mounted sinks have a number of advantages: they can be set at a height to suit your household, and they have covers to conceal pipes and waste traps available in finishes to match your faucets and are more aesthetically pleasing than conventional plastic versions. Alternatively, semi-inset sinks (the back fits into a piece of furniture or a shelf projecting from the wall) or inset units with self-rimming or undermounted sinks are available. The latter can be housed in cabinets with space for spare toiletries and cleaning materials. Although a boxed-in sink takes up extra visual and real space, it may provide enough storage to make the loss worthwhile.

Right An arrow-slit window of stained glass allows light from a hallway to illuminate a stainless-steel sink. Shelving "wings" and a towel rod underneath make clever use of a restricted space.

Below Tight in the corner, this sink is inset into a very small, floor-standing cupboard and has just enough room on top for faucets and water glasses. When not in use, it is hidden behind a folding storage door.

Above A small but elegant chrome faucet gives a classic look to this corner sink.

Left A sink with a tall spout set into the surround at the side makes optimum use of space. The mirror-fronted wall cabinet has accessible open shelving. Below, double doors conceal valuable storage space.

Above A smooth bowl of stainless steel, set below the faucet and water spout, has an almost clinical appeal that works well in this small space. The heated towel rod swings out into the room for easy access.

Below The sense of space is enhanced by banks of mirrored cabinets and by cubbyholes for storage and display. Stone-colored mosaic-tiled walls absorb the contours of the wall-mounted sink and faucets.

FAUCETS

Bathtubs and sinks are available with or without predrilled faucet holes, which means you have the option of installing faucets and pipes into the wall above, or into the surround. This frees up the area where the fixtures would usually be (and makes it easier to clean). It also means you can fix faucets at the middle rather than at the end of a bathtub, saving valuable space. And you may be able to enclose the tub in an alcove, with ceiling-height cabinets at either end, or keep both ends free for open shelving. Modern technology has also produced clean-lined fixtures that totally conceal plumbing, increasing visual space.

When faucets are smaller than average and set into the wall or surfaces around tubs or sinks, they merge with their surroundings, creating a streamlined effect. Faucets for sinks or tubs in compact single-lever designs take up less space than conventional faucets and often include pop-up drains. The ultimate in streamlined design is Philippe Starck's hand pump 10010: with its gently curved handle, it is the archetypal single-lever faucet. Concealed wall-mounted faucets are wonderfully neat and contained, just a circle of metal on a surface.

If everything else is hidden from sight – for example, in a completely tiled shower room – faucets will be the most conspicuous items on display, so choose the best quality you can afford.

Below A glass brick panel lets in light from the next room, illuminating the smart and practical color scheme created by setting white walls against blue mosaic tiles. The boxed-in cabinet conceals plumbing.

TOILETS

It makes sense in a small bathroom to try to contain the fixtures in as small an area as possible to free up vertical space for storage, or to "open up" the room with mirrors and panels of translucent glass that let light in. Both the gravity toilet and the pressure-assisted type are appropriate: there is no appreciable difference in size (although the latter is quieter and more efficient).

Back-to-wall toilets, where you can conceal a separate plastic tank behind a false wall, will save space. Bear in mind that the top of the concealed tank needs to have a certain minimum height above floor level to flush successfully. The false wall can often be used to recess other fixtures such as sinks, bidets, and wall-mounted towel rods. Building a false wall creates a useful shelf area above the fixture where bathroom accessories can be stored.

Enclosing the tank can provide extra storage space, as useful cabinets or rows of shelves may then be hidden behind the woodwork. Some toilets incorporate the tank and pan so they are reasonably contained. However, the height is preordained, and because they stand on the floor, valuable space may be used up or interrupted.

Above A curved false wall runs around the tub and under the window. This continues onto the adjoining wall to allow the toilet and sink to be wall-mounted, leaving the floor space free and creating a useful storage shelf.

Above Even in very small bathrooms, corners can be used to make the most of space. Here, a wedge-shaped tank, with mosaic tiling and a lid of slate that allows easy access to the plumbing, is used to cover the tank.

Right A wall-mounted toilet and sink are set on a false wall with a deep shelf on top and a mirrored wall above. The wall hides plumbing for the shower and wall-mounted faucets. A red panel on the right pivots for privacy.

DECORATING IDEAS
Images suggested by water and bathing offer a wealth of interesting visual, textural, and sensual ideas for bathroom accessories. Add touches such as shells arranged along windowsills, pieces of coral stacked on shelves alongside piles of clean towels, and baskets of ivory-colored soap mixed with pebbles from the beach, for example. However, with just enough room for fixtures, where do you display accessories in a small bathroom? If you decide to recess and wall-mount fixtures, shelf space can be created immediately above. Alternatively, if you carry on a false wall to ceiling height, recessed shelves can be built. If you set a bathtub into a mosaic-tiled surround, you can make a shelf around it or, if a tub fits neatly between walls, try placing display shelves at each end. Anything wall-mounted – radiators, towel rods, and so on – reduces clutter, as do the ingenious shower curtains that hold toiletries and soaps. Towel ladders mounted to or leaned against walls save space and add a contemporary touch.

Reflective finishes – shiny chrome and stainless steel – combined with semi-gloss paint bounce light off walls and enlarge the sense of space; larger mirrors and light colors on surfaces also help. Valuable space can be gained by rehanging the bathroom door so that it swings outwards instead of into the bathroom.

Far left Tongue-and-groove paneling is good for boxing in walls and fixtures in a bathroom. Here, the area at the back of the bathtub conceals the plumbing. A recessed box with glass shelves carries a neatly labeled collection of beach treasures. The area is illuminated by a light set in the top of the display box.

Left In this bathroom, good use has been made of the angled space below a large staircase. A built-in closet holds a washer and dryer, and at the end of the bathtub, the owner has used the slightly enclosed wall area to hold rows of open display shelves.

Above Neat cubbyholes make excellent storage and display spaces. Built into false walls, they integrate more smoothly and are far less obtrusive than wall-mounted racks and holders for various bathroom accessories.

WORKING

THE FRAMEWORK

New technology – desktop computers, the Internet, e-mail, and fax machines – means that more and more people are now able to work from home. Combined with changes in employment practices, which have led to a greater number of people becoming self-employed and doing freelance work, there is a greater need for home offices than ever before.

However desirable it may seem to have a separate workroom, a place to shut the door on at the end of the day without needing to clear everything away, in a small home this may simply not be viable. It is much more likely that your work area will be part of a dual-function space. If your home office is to be used for doing household paperwork and paying bills, and simply requires a table, chair, and a couple of files, there may be room in the hall, on a landing, or under the stairs. Alternatively, there may be a corner of the kitchen with room for a wall-mounted "shelf" table and stool.

If you need a more professional space, the first area to consider is usually the bedroom, which is generally unused during the day. Try to plan the space so that each function is as self-contained as possible. If the arrangement is intended to be long term, you will be best served by a bed that folds away completely out of sight. Sleeping and working require such different attitudes of mind that

Left A small study area in an apartment shared by a couple who do not work from home is hidden by a perforated aluminum blind that drops from a recessed slot in the top of the framework.

Right When the blind is raised, there is plenty of space for paperwork on the desk, reference books in the shelving cubes above, and audio equipment and CDs below. Clearance space has been allowed so that the chair can be placed under the counter when the blind is lowered.

if you are reminded of one while attempting the other, you may have difficulty relaxing or concentrating. If you can't fold the bed away, at least try to screen it off from the rest of the room. It is equally important to keep the work area – desk, computer, telephone, and files – out of sight when you are unwinding at the end of the day and preparing to go to sleep. Again, screening the area will help, but specially-designed space that can be completely closed off is definitely the best answer. A working "wall," with a work surface and space at the bottom for a chair, surrounded by storage cubes, drawers, and shelves, is ideal. Install doors that fold, slide, or simply open and close when the working day finishes. The same arrangement would work just as well in the living room, where the activities that take place are not so much at odds with each other as in the bedroom.

It's important to remember that working from home requires a different approach and frame of mind. Traditionally, the change to work mode is triggered when you leave home and set out for your place of employment. When you work from home, this no longer applies, so most people will find that it really helps to create a well-organized area where they can go to "switch on." Myriad attractive filing and storage systems are available to help you to make the most of your work space.

Far left Clever design turns what would have been wasted space on this attic bedroom wall into a desk that can be folded away when not in use. There is plenty of storage, too, in the cabinets on each side under the eaves, which are clad in white-painted boards. Using the same neutral tones everywhere in rooms such as this one helps to minimize the irregularity of the shape.

Left On the mezzanine floor of a city apartment, balcony guard rails create the framework for a small study desk. A metal shelving trolley is all the storage needed by a businessman who only occasionally works from home and limits his office equipment to a laptop computer and a telephone.

LIGHTING

Natural light is best for illuminating areas used during the day. Place your desk or table near a window if possible, to help energize, encourage, and enthuse flagging thought processes. Bear in mind, however, that computer screens should not be placed in front of, or facing onto, windows or other light sources since an uncomfortable glare can occur.

For workspaces without natural light, and for those times when artificial light is also needed, an overall ambient light, supplemented by strong direct adjustable lighting that can be positioned on the worksurface, is necessary. Gooseneck lamps are ideal. Designed to comply with the principle of form following function, the head and classic cantilevered structure can be maneuvered to shine in any direction. Current versions may be used with halogen bulbs to give a sharper and cleaner, more efficient light than the tungsten alternative. If space is really at a premium, there are versions of goosenecked and other desk lamps designed on similar lines that clip onto the sides or backs of counters or shelves. Floor lamps can give useful task lighting, too; there are designs available that twist, rotate, and extend as required. If your only source of light is a central fixture, extend the cable and put a hook in the ceiling above the work table to avoid the shadows caused when light flows from behind you.

Left This landing has floor-to-ceiling book-shelves on one side and a desktop housing a computer and printer on the other. During the day, light streams in through the two adjacent windows. By night, a gooseneck lamp illuminates the desk space.

Right A work area in the corner of a living room has a fabulous chrome floor lamp, which can be positioned directly over a computer keyboard.

Far right In this tiny office, created out of a vault under a city sidewalk, the architects introduced several ingenious ideas into the space, including a clever way of making a virtue out of the lighting cable. It snakes across the sloping ceiling to hang above the desk.

DESK AREAS

One of the advantages of working from home is that you have the freedom to decide on the furniture, accessories, and colors that will surround you. When choosing a desk, table, or work surface to be used on a daily basis, there are several guidelines worth following.

Sitting at a table for hours on end places pressure on the spine, so it is important to have the right chair. Chairs that fold down, such as director's chairs, are ideal in small spaces. If you have enough room, investigate office chairs, which are designed to support the back properly. They should be comfortable and allow your feet to rest on the floor with your knees slightly below hip level. Desktops are easy to improvise with MDF cut to size and painted. They can be wall-mounted to flip out and away as required. Alternatively, place them on sawhorses or a pair of filing cabinets. They should be high enough to allow your legs to fit underneath when your hands rest on the worktop and your elbows are bent at a 90-degree angle.

Where a home office is very much part of the living space, good organization and storage are not only efficient, they prevent the area from spreading and intruding into the rest of the room. Make sure that there is a place for everything, even if you just use a collection of baskets with tie-on labels for different bits of paperwork.

Far left A custom-built work space for a home-based businessman has shelves over the desk for folders, reference books, and papers used frequently; drawers under the desk store extra stationery. General lighting is recessed in the top of the framework, with a small adjustable lamp for added flexibility. When work is finished, a door slides down to hide the space from view.

Left In the corner of a busy family kitchen, a "shelf desk" is at the heart of the day-to-day running of the household. Calendar and telephone are at the ready on top, with a useful bulletin board above. A set of shelves over the desk holds telephone directories, magazines, and cookbooks.

SOLUTIONS

HEATING

If you live in one big room or in a small-scale house or apartment, standard forms of central heating and radiators can be problematic: in open-plan apartments, conventional radiators on outer walls rarely supply efficient heating; in small rooms radiators eat up valuable wall space. Radiant underfloor heating distributes warmth across whole rooms to maintain an even temperature throughout, and if you choose stone, ceramic, or wood floors, this is a worthwhile investment. It can be expensive, however, and whether you choose a wet or dry system, it needs to be installed professionally.

If you decide to use radiators, there are plenty of designs to choose from. Reproductions of classic cast-iron radiators, and the old-fashioned convector radiators, are available in tubular steel, aluminum, and copper and can be bought in small sections. Baseboard radiators, residential heating devices that run along the floor in place of a baseboard, are unobtrusive alternatives, as are commercial fin tube radiators, which are larger and more appropriate for industrial buildings. If space is really limited, a floor box radiator can be recessed into a trench in the floor and covered with a grill. Alternatively, you could opt for panel radiators. Stylish and barely visible, with the workings concealed at the back, they are expensive, but generate a powerful amount of heat from their surfaces.

Far left The small alcove in an entrance hall is just large enough for this classically designed tubular steel radiator. They are made to order in different sizes, colors and metallic finishes.

Left The use of open fires need not be limited to traditional interiors. For this apartment the architects designed a compact and graphic fireplace to hold a stylish steel basket with natural gas-fired coals.

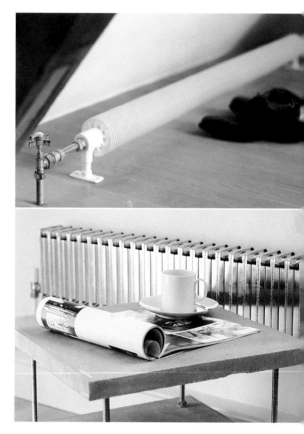

Top An elegant finned tube radiator was the perfect choice in this unusually shaped attic bedroom. It fits perfectly into the small vertical space created where the floor meets the angle of the roof.

Above A floor-mounted convector trench radiator has a chic and shiny modern design. These radiators can be purchased by length, depending on how much heat is needed in your particular space.

Right Neat, precise squares of light, recessed into the lower part of this staircase wall, illuminate the treads for safety and accent the warm tones of the natural wood stairs and the cinnamon-colored walls.

Far right Various sources of light working together create a painterly vista. Recessed ceiling fixtures are directed to illuminate artwork on the wall, and central recessed floor fixtures throw light up and around the wood-lined walls and ceiling to create the effect of a tunnel leading to a bright expanse.

LIGHTING

All too often lighting is only an afterthought, when it should be an important consideration from the outset. Effective lighting doesn't just provide for your functional needs; it makes the most of the aesthetics of a room, bringing life to colors, highlighting architectural details and textures, and lending atmosphere to a space.

Design the lighting in your home to create a variety of light levels for different functions. Built-in and recessed ceiling fixtures produce good general and background illumination. They need to be installed before you decorate to cause the least disruption, and they are a neat alternative to traditional overhead fixtures in small spaces as they don't intrude. When a whole area is illuminated, it opens up and appears larger. Recessed fixtures can also be angled to illuminate architectural features or paintings and work well when positioned just above the treads on staircase walls.

Inexpensive fluorescent tubes concealed at the top of a bookcase framework or shelf unit throw out a good level of light, and they provide the right countertop illumination when installed under kitchen cabinets. When lighting is mounted on a ceiling, with a screen below that does not cover the whole area, light washes out from the edges and floods the ceiling, making it appear higher than it is.

Top In a tiny cottage the architect set aside a small area at the ground-floor entrance, which leads off to a half-bath, for the laundry room. Three wooden panels elegantly screen the utility space off from the hall.

Bottom The central panel swings in as you enter and out as you leave. The appliances are lined up under a counter that also contains a sink. Above are cabinets to hold laundry detergent and other supplies.

LAUNDRY

Appliances and machines might make our lives run more smoothly, but seeing and hearing them is rarely life-enhancing. For most people, washing machines and dryers are household essentials, and they need to be easily accessible and, if possible, near a sink, with some nearby storage, counter, and hanging space. In larger homes, creating a utility room that can be closed off may be possible, but in smaller dwellings, kitchens or bathrooms are the most likely locations, although there may be space in a hall or under the staircase to fit laundry appliances.

Assessing and installing the right plumbing is obviously a priority, followed very closely by providing adequate ventilation. Washing machines and dryers are available in smaller-than-standard sizes, and certain models can be stacked on top of each other, thus using wall rather than floor space.

Where you choose to position these machines depends on how the rest of your space is organized. If your kitchen is open plan and designed to be the place where you eat (or if you work from home, where you meet with clients), whirring, spinning loads of laundry will be unacceptable here.

Above The laundry facilities in this apartment are in the bathroom, since the kitchen/living room is used for work. The cabinet doors reveal a washer and dryer below, with hanging space in the cubes on top.

Left The large stairwell in this urban apartment has been used to the full both for display and for storage in open cubes.

Right A hall has a discreet cupboard behind a door at the foot of the staircase. When the door is closed, the cupboard merges almost invisibly with the wall.

Far right The tiny room that used to house the central heating system offered a solution to the owner of this apartment who is passionate about fashion. Closets were built, with pigeonhole storage above for spare towels, bedding, and toiletries, and room for dozens of storage boxes to house an ever-increasing collection of shoes.

OVERFLOW STORAGE
Possessions can be divided into two categories: things we use regularly and things we use occasionally. They then break down into items that we'd prefer to hide away and those we are happy to display. Once these possessions have been placed in appropriate areas of use, where they can be most efficiently stored and accessed, there will inevitably be overflow.

Overflow includes items seldom used but needed at least once a year — seasonal clothes and shoes, books too tall to stack on built-in shelves, and even pictures that may be suitable for your next home, but aren't right for this one. It is all very well to be totally ruthless about getting rid of things in theory, but most of us are only prepared to go so far. So, in this tiny and ergonomically designed space, where is the overflow to go?

Niches of space created by architectural features, in particular staircases and understairs spaces, may provide a solution. Any available vertical space is always worth using up because it doesn't matter if items are out of reach: when things are seldom used or stored away for months, climbing a ladder to get to them won't be too much of a chore. Other dead spaces — below pitched-roof eaves, in small alcoves, or under windows — are alternatives, and, if your approach is both considered and imaginative, they can all be utilized.

SOURCES

Accessories

Bauerware
decorative knobs, pulls, and
handles
3886 17th Street
San Francisco, CA 94114
T (415) 864-3886
W www.bauerware.com

Chambers
bath products and bedlinens
T (800) 334-9790 for catalog

Smith + Noble
window coverings and blinds
1801 California Avenue
Corona, CA 91718
T (800) 426-8555 for catalog
F (800) 426-7780

Flooring

Country Floors
tile and stone floors
15 East 16th Street
New York, NY 10003
T (212) 627-8300

Foldaway furniture

Gloster Furniture
teak outdoor and folding
furniture
2195 Philpott Road
South Boston, VA 24592
T (877) GLOSTER (toll-free)
F (804) 575-1503

Roomax Space Beds
foldaway beds/wall beds
285 Industrial Way
Brisbane, CA 94005
T (415) 822-2337

Wall Bed Systems, Inc.
foldaway beds/wall beds
P.O. Box 2042
Wapakoneta, Ohio 45895
T (800) 413-4121
W www.wallbedsystems.com

Furniture

Design Centro Italia
contemporary home
furnishings
1290 Powell Street
Emeryville, CA 94608
T (510) 420-0383
W www.italydesign.com

Eclectica
contemporary and vintage
furniture
6333 West 3rd Street
Building 1200
Los Angeles, CA 90036
T (323) 634-5566

Evolution Furniture
contemporary and
convertible furniture
271 Ninth Street
San Francisco, CA 94103
T (415) 861-6665
W www.evolutionfurniture.com

Ikea
home furnishings
T (800) 434-4532 for store
locations or catalog

Mitchell Gold
upholstered and leather
seating
T (800) 789-5401 for catalog
W www.mitchellgold.com

Pottery Barn
home furnishings, house-
wares, and accessories
T (800) 922-5507 for store
locations or catalog

Glass Blocks

Pittsburgh Corning Corp.
glass blocks
800 Presque Isle Drive
Pittsburgh, PA 15239
T (800) 992-5769
F (412) 327-5890

Housewares

Crate and Barrel
housewares and accessories
T (800) 323-5461 for store
locations or catalog

Urban Outfitters
housewares, clothing, and
accessories
1801 Walnut Street
Philadelphia, PA 19103
T (215) 569-3131 for
store locations

Williams-Sonoma
gourmet kitchen products
T (800) 541-1262 for store
locations or catalog

Zona
housewares and accessories
97 Greene Street
New York, NY 10012
T (212) 925-6750

Industry information

**American Society of
Interior Designers**
interior design information
T (800) 775-ASID for
referrals worldwide
W www.interiors.org

**National Association of
the Remodeling Industry**
information and referrals
4900 Seminary Road, Ste. 320
Alexandria, VA 22311
T (703) 575-1100
F (703) 575-1121
W www.nari.org

Kitchens & bathrooms

American Standard
kitchen and bathroom
fixtures
T (800) 524-9797, ext. 356
for local dealers or brochure
W www.americanstandard-
us.com

C/S Bath
kitchen and bathroom
fixtures
566 Minnesota Street
San Francisco, CA 94107
T (800) 356-7473

Duravit USA (distributor of Philippe Starck designs) space-efficient kitchen and bathroom fixtures
1750 Breckinridge Parkway
Suite 500
Deluth, GA 30096
T (888) 387-2848
F (888) 387-2843
W www.duravit.com

Fox Marble & Granite
marble countertops
1400 Minnesota Street
San Francisco, CA 94107
T (415) 647-5160
F (415) 647-5163

Hansgrohe (distributor of Philippe Starck designs) kitchen and bathroom fixtures
T (800) 334-0455
W www.hansgrohe-usa.com

John Boos & Co.
maple countertops
315 South First Street
Effingham, IL 62401
T (217) 347-7701
F (217) 347-7705

KitchenAid
kitchen appliances
T (800) 541-6390
W www.KitchenAid.com

Kohler Co.
faucets and fixtures
T (800) 4KOHLER for local dealers or brochure
F (414) 457-1271
W www.kohlerco.com

KraftMaid
kitchen cabinetry
T (800) 581-4484 for dealers and brochure

Robern Home
space-efficient cabinets and fixtures
7 Wood Avenue
P.O. Box 2145
Bristol, PA 19007
T (800) 877-2376
W www.robern.com

The Bath & Beyond
kitchen and bathroom fixtures
135 Mississippi Street
San Francisco, CA 94107
T (415) 552-5001
F (415) 552-0714
W www.bathandbeyond.com

T.W. Murdock Co.
custom kitchen cabinetry
107 Parkhill Road
Sterling, VA 20164
T (703) 406-7511

Villeroy & Boch
kitchen and bathroom fixtures and tableware
T (888) 829-9090 or (800) 558-8453 for local dealers or catalog
W www.villeroy.com

Lighting

Lumisource
whimsical contemporary lighting
T (888) 461-5864 for local dealers or catalog
W www.lumisource.com

Radiators & heating

Edwards Engineering Corp.
radiators
101 Alexander Avenue
Pompton Plains, NJ 07444
T (800) 526-5201
W www.edwards-eng.com

Radiantec
underfloor heating
Box 1111
Lyndonville, VT 05851
T (800) 451-7593
W www.radiantec.com

Radiant Technology
radiant underfloor heating
11A Farber Drive
Bellport NY 11713
T (800) 784-0234 or (516) 286-0900
F (516) 286-0947
W www.radiant-tech.com

Staircases

J. di Cristina & Son
wood staircase designer
2745 16th Street
San Francisco, CA 94103
T (415) 431-8111

Safeway Stair Spiral Staircases
30 Pine Street
Stoneham, MA 02180
T (781) 438-4286
F (781) 279-0454
W www.safew.com

Storage

Blu Dot
shelving and storage units
1500 Jackson Street N.E.
Minneapolis, MN 55413
T (612) 782-1844
F (612) 782-1845
W www.bludot.com

California Closets
T (800) TOSIMPLIFY for locations nationwide
W www.calclosets.com

Hold Everything
storage products
T (800) 421-2264 for store locations or catalog

Stacks and Stacks
storage products
T (877) 2-STACKS
W www.stacksandstacks.com

INDEX

Page references in **bold** refer to illustrations

AEM **8–9**, 18–21, **46–7**
Ash Sakula 40, **41**

bathrooms **7**
  bathtubs 17, 94–5
  decorating ideas 89, 102–3
  display ideas **102**, 103
  faucets 89, **96**, 98–9
  fixtures 17, 89, **92**, 94–101
  lighting **90–1**, 92, **93**, **94**, 95, **96**, **97**
  on mezzanines 28, **29**, 36, **37**, **42–3**, **94**, 95
  plumbing **88**, 89, 96, 99, 100, **101**, **102**, 103
  showers 92–3, 95
  sinks 17, 96–9
  storage space 17, **94**, 95, **96**, **97**, **98**, **99**
  toilets 17, 100–1
bedrooms see sleeping areas
beds
  folding **7**, **8–9**, 36, **37**, 44, **72–3**, 74, 106
  raised **8–9**, **14–15**, 16, **17**, **46**, 74, **75**, 77
  screening 74
  size 77–8
  with storage space 11, **77**, 81
blinds **10**, 16, **106**
books 36, **42**, 44, 59, 106, **107**, **112**, 113
brick 21, **22**, 24
Broughton, Hugo **10–11**

cabinets
  for bathroom fixtures **97**, 99, **100**
  built-in **48**, 56, 78
  for kitchen appliances **53**, 56, **57**
  mirrored **98**, **99**
  for spare beds **7**
  for washing appliances 23, **24**, **102**, 103, **120**, **121**
  as window seats 60, **61**
CDs **43**, **48**, 106, **107**
ceilings **10–11**, **24–5**, **33**, 44, 118
chairs 35, 113
Circus Architects **7**, 14–17, 36, **37**, **56–7**, **78–9**
color
  for balance 21, **28–9**, **108**, 109
  and lighting 82
  for space creation **8–9**, **10–11**, 39, 60, 82, **88**, 89
  for zoning 17, **38–41**, **56–7**, 60–3, **76**, 77, **82–3**, **100**
concrete 40, **62**, 63
convertibility 6, **7**, **54–5**, 72–4, 106, 109
cooking equipment 52, 56, **58**, 59, 60, **61**, 64–5, **66**
countertops 23, 53–4, **58**, 59, 63, 65, **68**, 69

de Lisi, Ben 44–5, **82–3**
decorating ideas 39–41, 60–3, **78–9**, **82–3**, 89, 102–3
desks 28, **29**, **108**, 109, 112–13
dining areas
  with beds 36, **37**

convertibility 6, **7**, **54–5**
  in kitchens **64**, 65
  in living areas **7**, 32, **54–5**
dishware 56, **59**, 60, **61**, 64, 65, 66
dishwashers 25
display ideas 57–9, 66–9, **84**, 85, **102**, 103
Dolle, Adam **44–5**
doors
  folding **10**
  glass **20**, 21, **29**, 72, **73**, **90–1**
  sliding **20**, 21, 26, **27**, **38–9**, 92, **112**, 113
  wooden 24
dryers **24**, 121

electrical equipment 35, 36, **48**, **57**, 65

faucets 89, **94**, 95, **96**, 98–9
floor levels **7**, 36, **37**, **56–7**
floorplans **17**, **20**, **25**, **29**
food storage **53**, 54, 55, 66

galleries see mezzanines
glass
  ceilings **33**
  doors **20**, 21, **29**, 72, **73**, **90–1**
  panels **20–1**, 36, **37**, **38–9**, **76**, 77, **79**, 92
  partitions **48**
  roofs 40, **41**, **42–3**, 44
  sandblasted **48**
  shelving **21**, **102**, 103
  in showers **90–1**, 92–3
  stained 96, **97**
  tiles **16–17**, 92, **93**, **100**

walls 19, **20**, 21, **33**, **65**, 92, **93**, **100**
  see also mirrors
Granit 22–5, **42–3**, 60, **61**
granite **56**, 63

hallways 6, **25**, 28, **29**, 106
Hawkins Brown **32**, **33**, **34–5**
heating 116–17

kitchens
  clutter 56, **59**, 64–6
  decorating ideas 60–3
  dining areas **64**, 65
  display ideas 57–9, 66–9
  lighting **58**, 59, **65**, 66, 69
  screening **10**, **16–17**, **20–1**, 44, **45**, 53
  sinks 53
  storage space 17, **28–9**, 52–4, **56–9**, 60, **61**, 65

ladders **28–9**, 122
laundry areas 23, **25**, 28, **29**, **120–1**
lighting
  adapting 118–19
  ambient **48**, 110
  bathrooms **90–1**, 92, **93**, **94**, 95, **96**, **97**
  bedrooms 72, **76**, 77, **79**, 81, 82–3
  and color 82
  fluorescent **18–19**, 66, 118
  glass enhances **7**, **16–17**, 19, 21, **33**
  kitchens **58**, 59, **65**, 66, 69
  living areas **42**, 44, **45**, **47**, 48
  mirrors enhance 81, 82, **83**, 92, 93

natural **18–19**, 21, **64**, 65, 66, 110
  recessed **90–1**, **112**, 113, 118, **119**
  shelves **66**, **102**, 118
  task 35, **48**, 110, **111**, **112**, 113
  in working areas 110–11, **112**, 113
Littman Goddard Hogarth **38–9**, **54–5**, **72–3**
living areas
  with bedrooms 72–4
  convertibility **7**
  decorating ideas 39–41
  as dining areas **7**, 32, **54–5**
  lighting **42**, 44, **45**, **47**, 48
  storage space 36, 43

magazines 36, **44**
marble 63, **84**, 85, **94**, 95
materials
  for balance **22**, 24
  in bathrooms 89
  in kitchens **62**, 63
  patterned 40, **41**
  for space creation **10–11**, 16, 21, 74, **75**
  textured 40
  for zoning 40
  see also brick; glass; metal; stainless steel
metal
  in bathrooms 96, **97**, 103
  blinds **10**, 106
  shelves 66, **68**, 69
  staircases **8–9**, 16, **22**
  worktops **68**, 69
  see also stainless steel

mezzanines
  with bathrooms 28, **29**, 36, **37, 42–3, 94**, 95
  as design feature 11, **22**, 23, 44
  for sleeping 11, 36, **37, 42–3**, 74–5, 77
  as storage space 11, 26, **27**, 28, 77
  as working areas 11, 24, **25**, 36, **37**, 44, **108, 109**
microwaves 53, 56, **57**
mirrors
  on cupboards **98, 99**
  lighting enhanced 81, 82, **83**, 92, **93**
  recessed **90–1**
  as screens **7**
  in shelving 85
  for space creation 81, 92, **93**, 103
  as walls **101**

objets d'art 36, 84, **85**

paintings *see* pictures
panels
  glass 36, **37, 38–9, 76**, 77, **79**, 92, **100**
  sliding **20–1**, 28, **29**
partitions 47–8
pattern 40, **41**
pictures 36, 84, **85**
plumbing
  bathroom **88**, 89, 96, 99, 100, 101, **102**, 103
  laundry areas 121

radiators 103, 116–17
recesses
  bookshelves **44**

for display 11, **16**
mirrored **90–1**
for storage 11, **44, 90–1, 101, 102, 103**
for televisions 48, **49**
refrigerators 17, **25**, 53, 54
regulations 6, 16, 45, 47
roofspace 23, 24, 44, 72, **80, 81, 108, 109, 117**

screens
  beds hidden by **7**, 20, **38–9**, 74
  as design feature **16**
  to divide space 7, 47
  kitchens hidden **10, 16–17, 20–1**, 44, **45**, 53
  mirrored **7**
  workspace hidden **10, 106**, 109, **112**, 113
seating
  built-in **65**
  in kitchens **20**, 21, **54–5, 65**
  in living areas 35
  with storage space 11, **94–5**
  in working areas 106, **107**, 109, 113
shelves
  in bathrooms **100, 101, 102**, 103
  for display **20**, 59, 85, **102**, 103
  to divide space 36
  glass **21, 102**, 103
  kitchen 66–9
  lighting **66, 102**, 118
  metal 66, **68**, 69
  with mirrors 85

open 36, **44**, 59, 60, **61**, 66–9
recessed 11, **44, 90–1, 101, 102, 103**
window **66–7, 69**
showers **90–1**, 92–3, 95
shutters *see* panels
sinks **17**, 53, 96–9, **120**
sleeping areas
  clutter 85
  convertibility 6, 72, **73**
  decorating ideas **78–9, 82–3**
  in dining areas 36, **37**
  display ideas **84**, 85
  furniture 77–8
  on galleries 11, 36, **37, 42–3**, 74–5, 77
  lighting 72, **76**, 77, **79**, 81, 82–3
  in living areas 72–4
  screening **7, 20, 38–9**, 74
  storage space 77–8, 81, 82, **83**
  as working areas 72, 106, 109
sofas **29**, 35, 43–4
spare rooms 6, **7**, 36, **37**
stainless steel
  in bathrooms 96, **97**, 103
  in kitchens 26, 28, **62**, 63
  in living areas 40
  staircases **22**, 23, 24
stairs
  as design feature 23, **33**, 40, **41, 46, 47**, 77
  to divide space **47**
  lighting 118, **119**
  metal **8–9**, 16
  understair storage **8–9**, 11, 122

Starck, Philippe 96, 99
stereo equipment 20, 21, **48**, 106, **107**
storage space
  stereo equipment **20**, 21, **48**, 106, **107**
  bathroom 17, **94**, 95, **96, 97, 98**, 99
  for books 36, **42, 44**, 106, **107, 112**, 113
  built-in **48**, 56, 78
  CDs **43, 48**, 106, **107**
  for clutter 7, 36, 43–4, 64–6
  electrical equipment 36, **48, 57**
  food **53**, 54, 55, 66
  kitchen **17, 28–9**, 52–4, 56–9, 60, **61**, 65
  in living areas 36, 43
  on mezzanines 11, 26, **27**, 28, 77
  overflow 122–3
  in sleeping areas 77–8, 81, 82, **83**
  understairs **8–9**, 11, 122
  wall 7, **10–11**, 21, 122, **123**
stoves **25, 57**, 65
structural alterations 18, 44, 46, 77

tables 6, **28**, 32, 43, **54–5**
televisions
  recessed 48, **49**
  seating for 35
  on storage units **20**, 21, 26, 27, 28, 60, **61**
The Works 63
tiles **16–17, 22**, 24, **90–1**, 92, **93, 100**
toilets **17**, 100–1

walls
  glass 19, **20**, 21, **33, 65**, 92, **93, 100**
  mirrored **101**
  as storage space 7, **10–11**, 21, 26, 28, **53**, 122, **123**
  with workspace **108, 109**
washing machines 24, **102**, 103, 121
Wells Mackereth 26–9, **62–3, 90–1**
windows **25, 66–7**, 69
wood
  doors 24
  floors **8–9**, 16, 21, **22**, 23, 24, 40
  in kitchens **58**, 59, 63
  lighting **118–19**
  for space creation 16
  walls 44, **45, 102**, 103, **108, 109**
working areas
  in bedrooms 72
  case study 26–9
  convertibility 6
  decorating ideas **108, 109**
  desks 28, **29, 108**, 109, 112–13
  lighting 110–11, **112**, 113
  on mezzanines 11, 24, **25**, 36, **37**, 44, **108, 109**
  professional 106, 109, **112**, 113
  screening **10, 106**, 109, **112**, 113
  in sleeping areas 106, 109
  storage space **108**, 109

Author's acknowledgments

My thanks for their help and enthusiasm in finding locations for this book go especially to the following architects: Pascal Madoc Jones and Glyn Emrys at AEM Studio Ltd; Cany Ash at Ash Sakula Architects; Joanna Mehan at Granit Chartered Architects; Sally Mackereth at Wells Mackereth Architects; Vicky Emmett at Hawkins Brown Architects; Ian Hogarth at Littman Goddard Hogarth; Donnathea Bradford at Circus Architects. Thanks to all of the owners who allowed us to photograph their homes, especially Andrea Spencer, Pat Walker and Roger Hipwell, and Linda Farrow and Charlie Hawkins at The Works. Thanks also for excellent advice on use of colour to Judy Smith, Colour Consultant at Crown Paints, and for bathroom advice to Louis Saliman at CP Hart. The author would also like to thank Judith More, Janis Utton and Stephen Guise at Mitchell Beazley for most welcome encouragement, help and patience. Finally, a huge thank you to Dominic Blackmore for helping to find the locations and for taking such splendid photographs. ·